Exquisite Poems of a 7 Year Old

Remi Kou

BookLeaf Publishing

India | USA | UK

Presentation by *BookLeaf Publishing*

Web: www.bookleafpub.com

E-mail: info@bookleafpub.com

ISBN: 9789358314366

First edition 2023

To the Kou Shao Family

ACKNOWLEDGEMENT

Thank you to all the important people in my life.

The Fat Cat

My cat is very fat
But sometimes it holds a bat
My cat eats the bat
That makes it fat
But once it eats the bat
It eats a gnat
And then a rat

Feelings

When my mom is mad
It makes me sad
Because she cries
But her tears soon dry
Once her tears dry
She will always try
To not cry
In November
She cries
For December
In January
She cries
For February

Seasons

Spring is awesome
Spring is soggy
I love spring
More than anything
Autumn is dry
Which makes it beautiful
It is colorful and awesome
But then again
Spring is better than anything

The Five Senses

Your eyes help you see
Your ears help you hear
Your nose helps you smell
Your tongue helps you taste
Your fingers help you feel
Your body has these five senses
But some people do not
We need to help those people

Animal Adventures

I have a dog
He fell in a bog
And in that bog
There was another dog
They played and played
Until their energy faded away
Then my cow bowed
And my chicken
Met Charles Dickens

Candy and Chocolate

Chocolate is sweet and awesome
It is not bad for your teeth
Candy is sweet and awesome
But is bad for your teeth
Chocolate consists of milk
It can be dark, white, or caramel
Candy consists of sugar
It can give you cavities
This is my candy and chocolate theory

The Process of Eating a Candy

Sour and sweet
Candy
I put them in my mouth
Twirl it around my tongue
Touch my throat
Let it melt
Eat more
Savor the taste until next time

Minecraft

It is pixels
It is realistic
Dangerous sometimes
Or even cozy
Makes me feel at home
Calms me
Gems to mine, animals to breed, tools to craft
Endless worlds
Three dimensions, two portals
I want to play forever
When I stop, I am torn away from it
Can you guess what it is?

The Joy of Reading

Books have action
Books have suspense, even drama and history
Books give the world knowledge
Books have power within their words
Books transport you to another world
Books can grab you anytime
Books are amazing
Books are the best thing in the world
Books books books books books
You are holding one in your hand

Cookies

Cookies are sweet
Cookies are yummy
They fill your tummy
Cookies have chocolate
Cookies have sugar
They are different shapes and sizes
Cookies are delicious
Cookies make me drool
Cookies are the best
I crave for cookies

The Best Instrument in the World

It is brown
Comes with a bow
Bow has horsehair
Do not EVER touch the pegs
Makes beautiful sounds
It has feelings
When I hear it, I feel touched
I love playing it
It is a violin!

Mexico

Magical and magnificent
Eat tacos everyday every chance you get
Xylophone on the street playing upbeat music
International flights arriving every hour
Calavera everywhere during Dia de los Muertos
Opportunities to eat chips and guacamole

Corn

Wrapped in a green cloak
Peeled back, you will see whiskers on its head
Yellow, sweet, and on the cob
Turns into candy during Halloween
Appears as food on dinner plates
Found in farms and grows from the land
Starts small, soon grows big and tall
Turns into a maze in the Fall

Lego

Bumpy on the top
Smooth on the side
I feel pain when I step on it
It is satisfying when I put the pieces together
It can build many things
There are heads, bodies, and legs
You can build beautiful structures
You might have boxes of them
They clamp shut when put together
Always trying to think of a new thing to build
A square, a rectangle, a triangle
Maybe I could put the pieces together to make
an oval
So many adventures in my hands
Let's go to space!
Let's put out a fire!
What should I build next?

Tick Tock Clock

Everytime I ponder
What time is it?
I look up and see sixty numbers
There are three sticks
It's a clock!
Everytime I need a clock
To tell me, when should I do this? When should
I do that?
That's when my clock comes in handy
My clock is a circle, it is white, and it is hard
It has multiple numbers
Without my clock
I would not be able to know the time

My Pug

I had a pug
It ate a bug
It was very nasty
But my pug found it tasty
I looked up and saw
A thousand balls
They all fell
And landed in a well
I got a fan
Because I was boiling something in my pan
I used a spoon
To stir the pan at noon
I had not yet eaten lunch
My stomach felt like it had been punched
Then I went to see my friend
And told him…the end!

Cenote

Loud cheering
Super cold
Pit of water
In a cave
Black fishes swimming around
They touch my feet
I feel tingly
Looking up I see
Vines hanging
Water is very deep
Depth is two buses tall
People wearing life jackets
Diving around me
From a platform
Plopping and dropping
Natural wonder of Yucatan

The Heart of a Home

Sometimes when you are there
You will hear sizzling
Or boiling
There will be fantastic smells
You can make anything
After that you can eat it
Sometimes there are fires
And the use of water
You also use pots and pans
To create delicious dishes

Winter

Winter feels cold
But sometimes the snow is bold
All the leaves have fallen
It is colorless
It feels blank
When I look ahead I see miles of snow
You might feel abandoned
In the midst of the snow
You hear the clanging of icicles
When they fall from rooftops
The leaves have all blown away
Autumn is over
THIS IS WINTER!

16 Handles Froyo

When I walk in
I am greeted by a blast of chill
I feel delighted
When I walk up to the row of machines
I ask myself
Which combination should I get today?
Strawberry with vanilla
Chocolate with birthday cake
Orange creamsicle with graham cracker
I'll get that!
I take my first bite
There is a blast of flavor on my tongue
Brain freeze!
Let the good times swirl